50 STATES TO C

D0881875

Celebrating
COLORADO

www.hmhco.com

The text of this book is set in Weidemann.
The display type was set in Bernard Gothic.
The illustrations are drawn with pencil and colored digitally.
The maps are pen, ink, and watercolor.

Photograph of Rocky Mountain bighorn sheep on page 32 © 2011 by Corbis
Illustration of lark bunting on page 32 © 2011 by Houghton Mifflin Harcourt
Illustration of Rocky Mountain columbine on page 32 © 2011 by Houghton Mifflin Harcourt

Library of Congress Cataloging-in-Publication Data:
Kurtz, Jane.
Celebrating Colorado / written by Jane Kurtz ; illustrated by C.B. Canga.
p. cm. — (Green light readers level 3) (50 states to celebrate)
Audience: Grades K–3.
ISBN 978-0-544-51793-6 trade paper
ISBN 978-0-544-51794-3 paper over board
1. Colorado—Juvenile literature. I. Canga, C. B., illustrator. II. Title.
F776.3.K87 2016
978.8—dc23

Manufactured in China
SCP 10 9 8 7 6 5 4 3 2 1

4500573352

50 STATES TO CELEBRATE

Celebrating
COLORADO

Written by **Jane Kurtz**
Illustrated by **C. B. Canga**

Green Light Readers

Houghton Mifflin Harcourt

Boston   New York

COLORADO

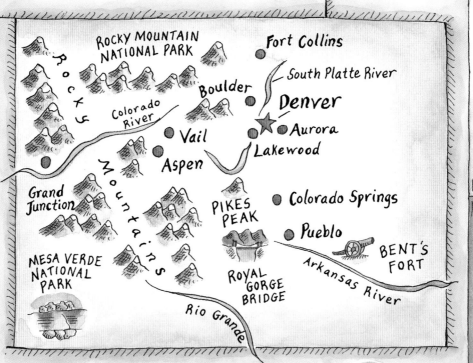

Rocky Mountains

ROCKY MOUNTAIN NATIONAL PARK

Fort Collins

South Platte River

Boulder

Denver

Colorado River

Vail

Aspen

★ Aurora

Lakewood

Grand Junction

Colorado Springs

PIKES PEAK

Pueblo

BENT'S FORT

MESA VERDE NATIONAL PARK

Arkansas River

ROYAL GORGE BRIDGE

Rio Grande

N W E S

Hi. I'm Mr. Geo.
I'm in a state full of
majestic mountains,
golden fields,
and giant red rocks.
Colorful Colorado!

The name Colorado comes from the Spanish word for "colored red" (*color rojo*).

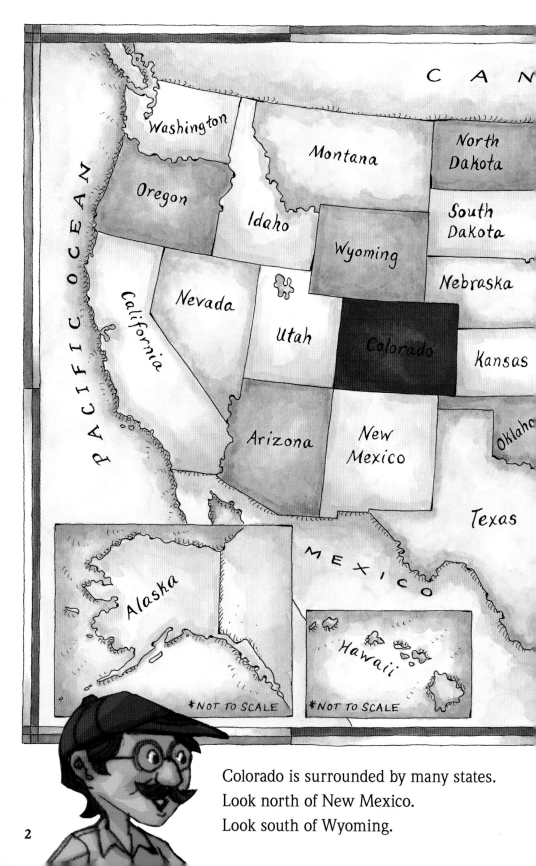

Colorado is surrounded by many states.
Look north of New Mexico.
Look south of Wyoming.

2

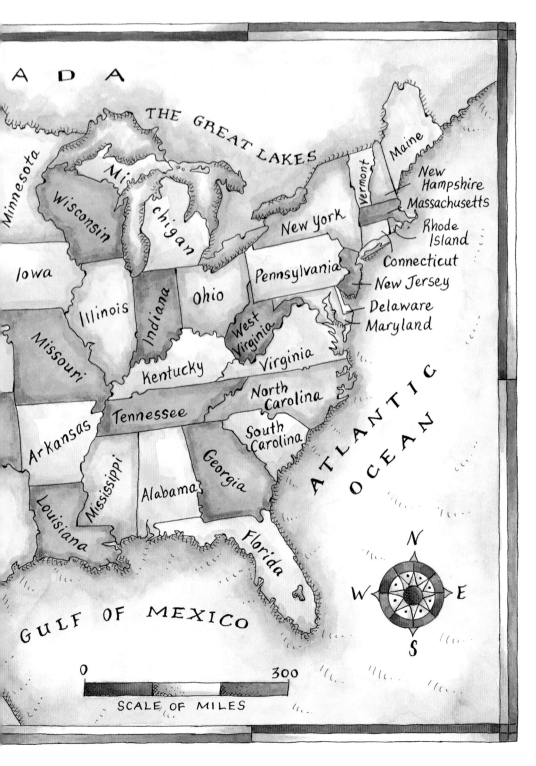

Look east of Utah.

Look west of Kansas and Nebraska.

Can you spot Colorado?

Ready to climb up 14,000 feet?
Don't worry!
This train does all the chugging.
It's heading to the top of
Pikes Peak.

Pikes Peak is named for the explorer
Zebulon Pike.

The **landscape** and weather
change as we go up.
The types of animals change too.
I'm glad I'm not in the middle
of that bighorn ram **rumble**.

High up on Pikes Peak,
the view amazes me!
It's oh so beautiful.

After a visit to the top of Pikes Peak in 1893, Katharine Lee Bates wrote the words to the song "America the Beautiful."

Spacious blue skies.

Purple mountain peaks

high above fields and **plains.**

Tasty donuts, too!

Donuts have been served atop Pikes Peak since 1916. It takes a special recipe to make them at such a high **altitude.**

Colorado is home to many parks.
Rocky Mountain National Park
is my favorite for horseback riding.
Whoa!
Let's stop and smell the blossoms.

Colorado has more than 50 mountains that are greater than 14,000 feet high. Hikers call them "fourteeners."

Way up at the top of Trail Ridge Road,
the rocks look like mushrooms.
Listen to that yellow-bellied **marmot**!
No wonder people gave it the nickname
"whistle pig."

Did you know?

Other animals in Rocky Mountain National Park include elk, eagles, mule deer, moose, mountain lions, and coyotes.

Today we're visiting
Great Sand Dunes National Park and Preserve.
We can see **bison** drinking at Dollar Lake.
We can sand sled down the giant **dunes**.
What I love best is cooling off at
Medano Creek.

Now let's visit Picketwire Canyonlands.

We can stroll among huge dinosaur footprints.

How does my foot measure up?

Mesa Verde National Park thrills me too.
The Ancestral Pueblo lived here long ago.
They built homes into the side of the cliffs.
I crawled and climbed to this Balcony House.
How did the builders do it?

There are also cliff dwellings near Manitou
Springs, Colorado.

In later times, the Ute people lived in **tepees**.

They hunted in the mountains and plains.

We can still see their rock art.

I wonder where that horse is going.

Did you know?

The first Europeans in Colorado were Spanish explorers. They brought the first horses to the area.

In the 1800s, Mountain Men came
to hunt beaver and trade fur.
This **reenactment** shows us ways
they lived and did business.
It's my turn in the frying pan event.
Ready, set, toss!

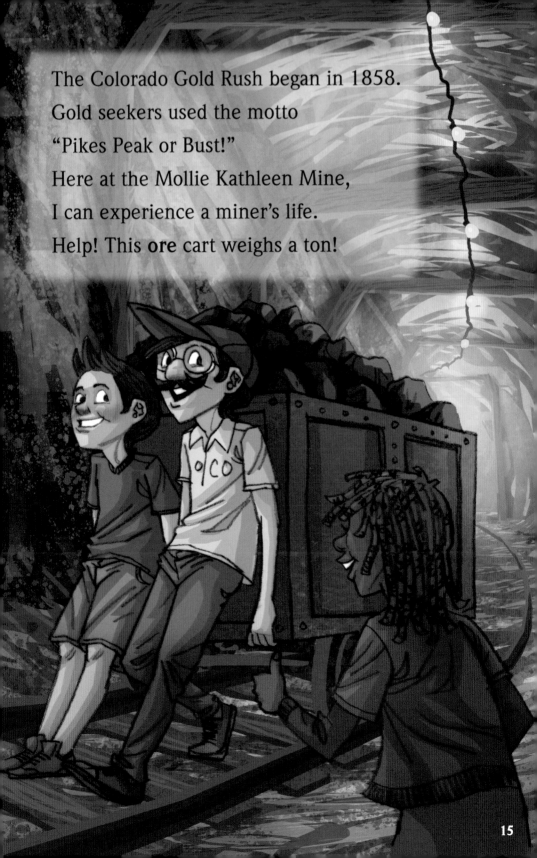

The Colorado Gold Rush began in 1858.
Gold seekers used the motto
"Pikes Peak or Bust!"
Here at the Mollie Kathleen Mine,
I can experience a miner's life.
Help! This **ore** cart weighs a ton!

Now I am at Bent's Fort.
Covered wagons like this
carried pioneers west.
"All's set!" Let's explore the Santa Fe Trail.

Ranches grew huge in early Colorado.

Hundreds of cowboys herded cattle.

Many are still hard at work here.

I'm learning how to lasso at this dude ranch.

But I'm not ready for a roundup yet!

Denver hosts one of the world's largest rodeos, the National Western Stock Show.

In these mountains and valleys,
people love living the outdoor life.
Me too!
I bike all over Boulder.

Now I am trying rock climbing.
But I'm not sure if I'll do it again.
The **canyon** walls are so steep!

I love hiking up
the mountains of Colorado.
But I can't wait
to come back in winter . . .

Then I will ski my way down!
Woo-hoo!

 **Did you know?**

Vail, Aspen, Snowmass, Keystone, Winterpark, Steamboat Springs, and Telluride are among the many ski resort areas in Colorado.

Sometimes I like to relax
while the pros play sports.
But not now . . .
the Rockies just loaded the bases!
Time to rally!

Did you know?

Basketball fans in Colorado cheer for the
Denver Nuggets, and hockey fans follow
the Colorado Avalanche.

Colorado fans also love their Broncos.
The team plays in a stadium
that's a mile high.
I'm getting the grand tour today.

The Denver Broncos won back-to-back Super
Bowl championships in 1997 and 1998.

Different types of businesses make
Colorado's **economy** strong.
The plains are great for raising cattle and sheep.
Farming, too!

Colorado's top vegetable crops are potatoes,
cabbage, and onions. The top fruit crops are
peaches, apples, and cantaloupe.

Colorado mountains have precious resources,
including **minerals, petroleum,** and **coal.**
At the National Mining Hall of Fame,
I saw colorful crystals and precious metals.
I liked this bronze statue the most!

Minerals are important for making many
household products, including toothpaste,
shampoo, glassware, and plastic bottles.

Colorado cities are full of attractions.
Let's climb to the thirteenth step
of the state capitol in Denver.
It's exactly one mile above sea level.
This is the Mile High City!

ONE MILE ABOVE SEA LEVEL

Did you know?

The gold on the capitol's sparkling dome
comes from Colorado mines.

Denver has many lovely parks.

It has lots of beautiful museums.

But my favorite spot to see art is outside.

I see you too, Big Blue Bear!

Let's head south next.

I've always wanted to visit Royal **Gorge**.

Some like to see it from the top down.

But I love to see it from the bottom up.

Did you know?

The Royal Gorge Bridge is the highest bridge in the United States. It hangs 956 feet above the Arkansas River.

There's lots to do in nearby Colorado Springs.
Caves, waterfalls, and hot springs!
My favorite place is the
U.S. Olympic Training Center.
Gymnasts flip and leap.
I'm inspired to try too!

I'm ending my trip with a stroll
around Garden of the Gods.
Soaring spires of red rock make me
wonder how soon I can come back
to colorful Colorado.

Fast Facts
About Colorado

Nickname: Centennial State, Colorful Colorado

State motto: Nothing without providence

State capital: Denver

Other major cities: Colorado Springs, Aurora, Fort Collins, Lakewood

Year of statehood: 1876

State mammal:
Rocky Mountain bighorn sheep

State bird: Lark bunting

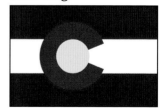

State flower:
Rocky Mountain columbine

State flag:

Population: 5.4 million, according to the 2013 U.S. Census

Fun fact: The Four Corners area of Colorado is where the borders of Colorado, Utah, Arizona, and New Mexico meet.

Dates in Colorado History

Circa 1100: Ancestors of the Pueblo begin building cliff houses at Mesa Verde.

1776: Spanish explorers map the Colorado Plateau.

1806: Zebulon Pike sees the mountain that will become Pikes Peak.

1821: William Becknell establishes the Santa Fe Trail from Franklin, Missouri, to Santa Fe, New Mexico, through parts of southeast Colorado.

1848: The land of present-day Colorado goes from Mexican to United States control.

1858: The Pikes Peak Gold Rush begins.

1870: The Kansas Pacific Railroad reaches Denver.

1876: The Atchison, Topeka, and Santa Fe Railroad reaches Pueblo.

1893: Katharine Lee Bates visits Pikes Peak and is inspired to write "America the Beautiful."

1906: The ancient cliff dwellings at Mesa Verde become a part of a national park.

1915: Rocky Mountain National Park and Dinosaur National Monument are established.

1932: The Great Sand Dunes are named a national monument.

2007: Colorado adopts "Rocky Mountain High" by the singer-songwriter John Denver as one of its state songs. The song celebrates the joy Colorado's natural beauty and outdoor resources inspire.

Activities

1. **LOCATE** the six states that border Colorado on the map on pages 2 and 3. Which states are to the north? Which states are to the south? Which state is to the east? Which state is to the west? SAY the name of each state that borders Colorado out loud.

2. **DRAW** a picture of rock art that depicts something about Colorado. On the back, explain why you created the design.

3. **SHARE** two facts you learned about Colorado with a family member or friend.

4. **PRETEND** you are hosting a TV travel show about Colorado. During the show the audience asks you questions. Answer the following questions correctly so your show gets great ratings and you can keep traveling to more places in the United States to do more TV shows. Good luck!

   a. **WHO** wrote "America the Beautiful"?

   b. **WHAT** animal is nicknamed "whistle pig"?

   c. **WHEN** did the Pikes Peak Gold Rush start?

   d. **WHICH** city in Colorado is home to an Olympic Training Center?

5. **UNJUMBLE** these words that have something to do with Colorado. Write your answers on a separate sheet of paper.

   a. **KIPSE KPAE** (HINT: a mountain)

   b. **BSONI:** (HINT: a big animal)

   c. **NRHCA** (HINT: where cattle are raised)

   d. **IGSIKN** (HINT: a winter sport)

FOR ANSWERS, SEE PAGE 36.

Glossary

altitude: a distance above sea level or above the earth's surface. (p. 7)

bison: a large hoofed animal of western North America that has a shaggy, dark brown mane and short, curved horns; bison are sometimes called buffalo. (p. 10)

canyon: a deep valley with steep, rocky walls on both sides. Canyons are formed when rivers or streams wash away soil and rock over a long period of time. (p. 19)

coal: a solid black substance that is mined from the earth and used for fuel; it can be used to power a factory or cook food on a grill. (p. 25)

dune: a hill or ridge of sand that the wind has piled up. (p. 10)

economy: the way a community of people uses resources to produce goods and services. (p. 24)

gorge: a deep narrow valley with very steep sides. (p. 28)

landscape: an area or stretch of land that is viewed as scenery. (p. 5)

majestic: grand, large, and very fine in appearance. (p. 1)

marmot: a short-tailed burrowing animal with a bushy tail (p. 9)

mineral: a natural, nonliving substance that is mined for human use; examples of minerals include gold, silver, copper, and zinc. (p. 25)

ore: rock that is removed from the earth in order to get a valuable substance that is in it; ore is the source for metals such as iron, gold, silver and copper. (p. 15)

petroleum: a thick, yellowish-black oil that occurs naturally below the surface of the earth. (p. 25)

plain: a large flat area with few trees. (p. 7)

reenactment: an occasion on which people reenact an event; the event is often of historical importance. (p. 14)

rumble: a fight or brawl; rumble also means to roar, thunder, or boom. (p. 5)

spacious: roomy, wide open, or expansive. (p. 7)

tepee: a large tent that is shaped like a cone, made of long wooden poles with a cover of animal hides or canvas; some Native American people once lived in tepees. (p. 13)

Answers to Activities on page 34:

1) Wyoming and Nebraska are to the north (Nebraska is also to the east); New Mexico and Oklahoma are to the south; Kansas and Nebraska are to the east (Nebraska is also to the north); Utah is to the west; 2) Drawings will vary; 3) Answers will vary; 4a) Katharine Lee Bates, 4b) marmot, 4c) 1858, 4d) Colorado Springs; 5a) Pikes Peak, 5b) bison, 5c) ranch, 5d) skiing.